One of the very last trolleybuses to enter service was Bournemouth Corporation 301, a Sunbeam MF2B.

OLD TROLLEYBUSES

David Kaye

Shire Publications Ltd

CONTENTS

Printed in Great Britain by C. I. Thomas & Sons (Haverfordwest) Ltd, Press Buildings, Merlins Bridge, Haverfordwest, Dyfed.

British Library Cataloguing in Publication Data available.

Cover: *Huddersfield Corporation 631, a Sunbeam S7 with East Lancs bodywork, in service at a Sandtoft 'Trolleyday'.*

ACKNOWLEDGEMENTS

I should like to thank all those who have helped make this Album possible, and especially Michael Fowler, who provided me with such a wide variety of illustrations.

Photographs are acknowledged as follows: J. Barley, pages 15, 21 (lower right); H. Brearley, pages 5 (upper), 6, 7 (lower), 10 (lower); British Transport Commission, page 26 (lower); N. Brook, pages 5 (lower two), 9; W. Cable-Scott, page 10 (upper); C. Carter, page 24 (upper); M. J. C. Dare, page 19 (lower); East Anglia Transport Museum, page 28; M. Fowler, pages 11, 13, 14, 16, 17, 18 (upper), 20, 21 (upper), 23, 24 (lower); M. Greenwood, page 30; D. Kaye, pages 7 (upper), 8, 19 (upper), 22, 25 (upper), 26 (upper), 27, 29; Leeds City Transport, page 4; London Transport, page 3; R. C. Ludgate, page 18 (lower); R. F. Mack, page 12 (top and centre); Photofive, page 12 (bottom); R. D. H. Symons, page 21 (lower left); Yellow Coaches, page 25 (upper).

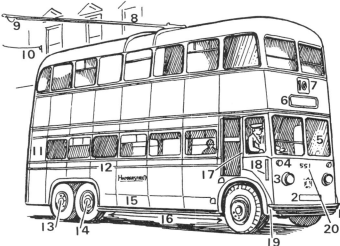

Diagram of a 1948 six-wheeler trolleybus (front offside view). Key to numbered parts: 1 chrome strip front bumper; 2 registration number plate; 3 headlamp; 4 side light; 5 front bulkhead (in this case enclosed within the 'fully fronted' bodywork); 6 destination blind; 7 route number blind; 8 trolley booms; 9 trolley heads on overhead; 10 span wire attached to wall bracket; 11 enclosed rear staircase with luggage compartment beneath; 12 waist band; 13 live axle (driving axle); 14 trailing axle; 15 battery compartments; 16 wheelbase; 17 sliding cab door; 18 trafficator; 19 front wing; 20 fleet number.

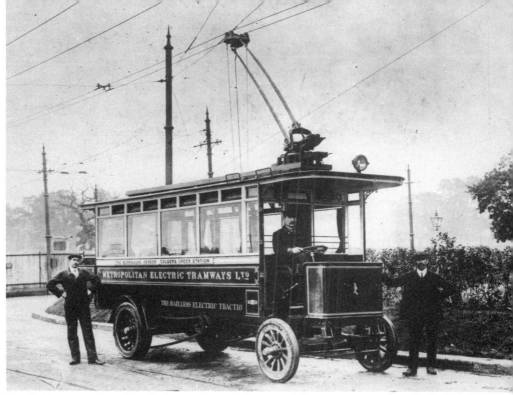

The Railless experimental trolleybus at the 1909 Hendon trials.

THE EXPERIMENTS

It was on 29th April 1882 in a Berlin suburb that Dr Ernst Werner von Siemens tried out the world's first trolley-bus. It took the form of a modified horse-drawn wagonette fitted with a pair of 3 horsepower electric motors which drove the rear wheels by means of a chain. The current came from twin overhead wires on which ran a small eight-wheeled trolley. An extant photograph shows that its rear wheels had approximately twice the diameter of those at the front. The trolley was connected to upright poles in the centre of the vehicle by a flexible cable. This experiment lasted for 5½ weeks, terminating on 13th June.

Eighteen years later came the next experimental vehicle, designed by the Frenchman Lombard Gérin for the Paris Exhibition of 1900. In the following year Max Schiemann started the world's first

fare-paying trolleybus service in Bielathal in his native Germany on 10th July. Whereas Siemens' trolley had run on top of the wires, Schiemann's ran under them, a system that eventually became universally adopted. The Austrian firm of Cedes-Stoll operated an articulated trolleybus in Dresden as early as 1902. Later they installed a greatly improved model in Vienna. This was driven by electric motors installed in the hub of each wheel. It pulled a trailer, enabling twice as many passengers to be carried. In Italy La Societa per la Trazione was running a route 25 km (15½ miles) long near Milan before 1910.

Electrically powered public service vehicles in Britain date back to January 1889 with the founding of the Ward Electrical Car Company to build and operate electric battery buses. But it was

Two of the Railless single-deckers which inaugurated the Leeds system in June 1911.

not until 7th July 1908 that the concept of the trolleybus began to become a reality in Britain with the registration of the Railless Electric Traction Company. In November of that year Dodd and Dodd of Birmingham announced plans to install a trolleybus system in the fashionable spa town of Malvern with its steep gradients. The following week the Dalkeith Railless Electric Car Company reported that they intended to run a service with departures every ten minutes between their base and Edinburgh using six 34-seat trolleybuses. None of these schemes was put into effect, nor were there any better results later at Birkenhead, where Britain's first trolleybus ran under tramway wiring in 1909. Birkenhead was also the scene of the first British tram trials in 1860. For 2½ hours on the morning of Saturday 25th September 1909 Londoners had an opportunity to view this Railless vehicle with its 22-seat Milnes Voss body at Hendon, where it ran under Metro-

politan Electric Tramways colours. But there were no orders for trolleybuses for a further 22 years. A second London area experiment was staged at West Ham in 1912.

The honour of becoming the real pioneers in this mode of transport in Britain belonged jointly to Bradford and Leeds, which began their public services simultaneously on 20th June 1911. Bradford's later extensive use of trolleybuses was not apparent in this initial enterprise since it bought only two trolleybuses while its neighbour invested in four. All six were built by Railless and powered by twin 20 horsepower Siemens motors of 525 volts DC, which drove the rear wheels by chain and sprocket. The bodies were of 28-seater single-decked construction by Hurst Nelson.

By the outbreak of the First World War on 4th August 1914 there were seven separate networks in Britain, the new-comers being those at Aberdare, Keigh-

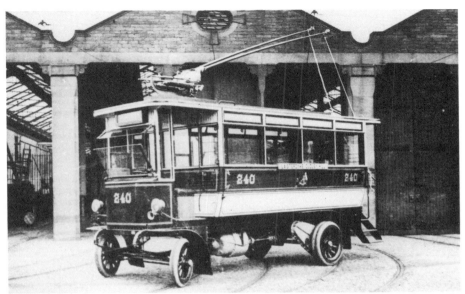

One of Bradford Corporation's first pair of Railless single-deckers, showing their chain drive to the rear axle.

The crew of Bradford 514 (built by the operator) pose for the camera on the Oakenshaw route in the 1920s.

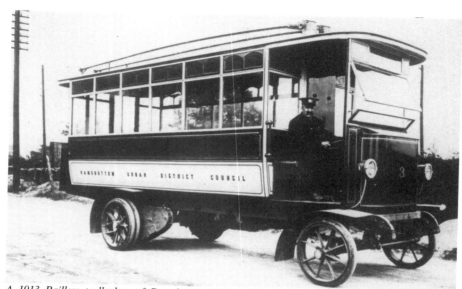

A 1913 Railless trolleybus of Ramsbottom Urban District Council with its booms lowered.

ley, Ramsbottom, Rotherham and Stockport. However, even by that early date there had been one casualty, Dundee, whose short route operated only from 5th September 1912 until 13th May 1914. It was to be another 35 years before trolleybuses ran once more in Scotland. The Aberdare and Keighley systems used the Cedes-Stoll method of current collection, whereby a flexible cable (balanced by a pendulum) joined the trolley and the vehicle. This necessitated the exchange of trolleys when vehicles needed to pass one another — a cumbersome and time-consuming operation. On the other hand, Stockport employed the Lloyd-Köhler method in which the negative wire was mounted immediately above the positive wire instead of beside it as in the Schiemann and Cedes-Stoll systems. The two-wheeled trolley rode on the negative wire, whilst a spring-loaded bow collector travelled on the lower wire.

All these early vehicles had been single-deckers, their bodies being largely based on those of the tramcars of Edwardian days. Not surprisingly they were often referred to as 'trams'. Alternative titles invented for them during this initial period included 'trackless trolley' and 'trolley omnibus', although as early as 1909 a writer in *Commercial Motor* had chosen their eventual name, 'trolleybus'. Indeed, in their first decade of operation even the government thought of them as trams since no road fund licences were required to operate them and therefore they bore no registration plates.

Nevertheless there were experimental double-deckers around. One was a Cedes-Stoll with a 34-seat Dodson body which was tried out in the middle of September 1914 by Hove Corporation on a specially erected section of overhead wiring between Church Road and Hove station. But this select seaside resort decided not to purchase any. Eventually, in 1917, this same vehicle entered regular service with Keighley Corporation. Earlier, in December 1913, a double-decker of similar size, made entirely by Railless, was tried out by Brighton Corporation between St Peter's church and Rose Hill Terrace. This time trolleybuses were eventually ordered — but not until 1939!

During the First World War two more systems were opened: a short-lived one was started in the Rhondda on 22nd December 1914 and another which lasted much longer, at Mexborough and Swinton on 31st August 1915. These were the

An early Mexborough and Swinton Daimler trolleybus with a 28-seat Brush body.

Four Railless trolleybuses were employed by York City for its first short-lived trolleybus network.

The unique Bradford Corporation twin-steer double-decker, designed and built by the corporation in 1922.

Wigan Corporation number 1 worked on a small system that lasted only from 1925 to 1931.

UM 1755 was the Garrett 'S' type prototype. Built for Leeds City, it was employed as a demonstrator before entering the fleet at Bradford as number 536.

first to be operated by private companies rather than by municipal authorities. Soon after the Armistice was signed work began on the Tees-side network, jointly owned by Middlesbrough Corporation and Eston Urban District Council. This opened on 8th November 1919 and was one of the longest lasting systems in Britain. York began the first of two brief attempts to run trolleybuses in 1920, followed by another ephemeral system in hilly Halifax (1921-6). On 27th November 1922 trolleybuses were introduced to Birmingham for the first time.

The decision by the Ipswich engineering firm of Ransomes, Sims and Jefferies to build vehicles of this kind had a considerable impact on the future of trolleybus transport. Garrett of Leiston, also in Suffolk, followed suit. Both these manufacturers designed trolleybuses that had few links with the tram and more with the rapidly developing motorbus. Indeed, when Leyland and AEC entered this field at the end of the decade their first products looked exactly like motorbuses, down to the fitting of the standard 'Titan' or 'Regal' radiator at the front of the vehicle.

1920 to 1930 was still largely the era of the single-decker trolleybus: the Garrett 'O' type, the Guy BT 32 and the Ransomes, Sims and Jefferies vehicles. They were bought by many of the new systems which commenced operations from 1925 onwards, such as Wigan (May 1925), Grimsby (October 1926), Chesterfield (July 1927) and Hastings (January 1928).

However, the double-decker was finding favour in other areas. Bradford had built the first of its own double-deckers in 1920. Compared with contemporary motorbuses that normally seated 46 passengers, the trolleybus of the same dimensions, because of the absence of a large forward-positioned petrol engine, could seat up to six more. Two years later Bradford built its unique twin-steer double-decker with two front axles, an idea that was repeated only once more, by London Transport in 1939, when it placed into service the sole Leyland 'Steer' trolleybus. Some systems were re-equipped with double-deckers as the first generation of vehicles wore out. Keighley did this between 1924 and 1926, buying ten Straker-Cloughs. With the advent of the extended chassis of 26 or 27 feet (7.5 or 7.9 metres), Guy introduced its BTX60 and BTX66 models that had

9

two rear axles (obeying the legal requirements of that time) and seated 60 or 66 passengers respectively. This was followed by the similar Karrier E6. These were ideal for the new networks being constructed in Doncaster (1928), Nottingham (1926) and Wolverhampton (1926). These double-deckers all had roofed-in top decks, unlike many of the motorbuses and electric tramcars of this period.

This was the beginning of an accelerating process of removing tramways from Britain's towns and cities. Although in some cases motorbuses replaced trams (as in Burton-on-Trent, Colchester, Gosport, Lincoln and Swindon), in other towns trams were succeeded by trolleybuses (as in Darlington, Ipswich and West Hartlepool).

Left: *Hastings Tramway Company bought some Guy BTX double-deckers with Dodson open-top bodies in 1927, of which this one (nicknamed 'Happy Harold') has survived.*

Below: *When the City of York reopened its trolleybus system in 1930, it was equipped with three Karrier E4s, of which number 30 was one.*

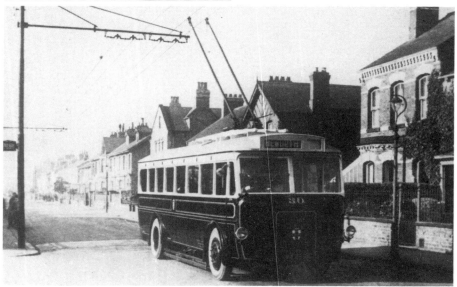

The six-wheeler version of the Karrier E4 was the E6, of which Huddersfield Corporation 493 was one, here seen en route for Marsden in 1962.

THE HEYDAY IN THE 1930s

The decade from 1930 to 1940 saw the wholesale abandonment of trams in favour of either the new generation of motorbuses (including, in the second half of this period, the more efficient and economical diesel-engined vehicles) or trolleybuses. They, too, had a new look compared with their predecessors and had more powerful motors which enabled them to tackle almost any terrain, thus bringing swift and virtually silent public transport.

No expansion of trolleybus services was more dramatic than that which took place in London, especially after the establishment of the London Passenger Transport Board in 1933. This body immediately decided to substitute trolleybuses for the variety of aging tramcars which it had inherited from the various undertakings that had been taken over by the board. The outbreak of the Second World War halted this process, but by 1952 the London fleet had built up to 1811 vehicles, by far the most extensive and intensive network in the world. It was even anticipated at one stage that the famous and unique Kingsway tram subway would be converted for use by trolleybuses and to that end an experimental vehicle (1379) was built with an offside platform to cope with the centrally positioned platform in the middle of the underpass. However this plan was never implemented as the motorbuses which replaced the trams used Kingsway and Aldwych instead of travelling underground to the Embankment.

The first London trolleybuses were placed into service by London United Tramways on 16th May 1931. The unusual looking AEC 663Ts had flat fronts with distinctive centrally mounted bullseye headlamps and earned the quaint nickname of 'Diddlers'. The first route was between Twickenham and Teddington, followed by a small network of routes in the Hounslow and Kingston upon Thames areas. These places were relatively flat: the 1 in 9 gradient of Anerley Hill, negotiated by the service up to the Crystal Palace, necessitated the fitting to the vehicles of special runback brakes.

Above: *Grimsby Corporation 21 with Roe bodywork was a typical example of the AEC 661T of the 1930s.*

Left: *Another example of the AEC 661T was Portsmouth Corporation 233 with Craven bodywork, seen here passing Portsmouth town railway station in 1959.*

Below: *A model of a London Transport F1 class Leyland LPTB70 trolleybus of 1937.*

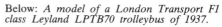

London Transport class L3 consisted of AEC-MCW chassisless vehicles like 1514, built at the beginning of the Second World War. This trolleybus was photographed at Wimbledon.

As in the previous decades, by no means all towns replaced their trams with trolleybuses. For example, in 1931 alone Ayr, Cork, Exeter and Scarborough all substituted motorbuses, only Pontypridd continuing with electric transport in the form of trolleybuses. Amongst the larger networks which were established in the 1930s were Walsall (1931), Derby (1932), Huddersfield (1933), Bournemouth and Portsmouth (1934), Newcastle upon Tyne (1935), Reading (1936), Kingston upon Hull (1937), Belfast and Manchester (1938). Amongst the new systems were two inter-urban companies. South Lancashire Transport had 35 route miles (56.3 km) including a service 14 miles (22.5 km) long between Atherton and Farnworth. Notts and Derby Traction Company (a subsidiary of Midland General Omnibus Company) covered 26 route miles (41.7 km), including the long run from Ripley into the centre of Nottingham. The final conversion from trams to trolleybuses during this decade was made by Brighton Corporation on 31st August 1939, just three days before the outbreak of the Second World War,

which prevented its partner in this scheme, Brighton, Hove and District Omnibus Company, from placing its own vehicles into service. AEC 661Ts had to be stored until government permission was granted for their introduction in 1944.

By 1936 there were other manufacturers trying to cash in on the expanding trolleybus market. Sunbeam had started in 1931, whilst English Electric (which had been manufacturing electric motors for trolleybuses for some years) began building complete trolleybuses (including the bodies) in 1932. In 1936 two well established motorbus manufacturers, Crossley and Daimler, also started to build these electric vehicles. For Daimler it was its second entry into this field. Even Bristol made a half-hearted attempt to join in this lucrative market.

The vogue for streamlined transport, which could be seen in the second half of this decade on the railways and on the race track, also had its influence on the bodywork designed for trolleybuses. Sometimes this trend was emphasised by the livery adopted, as in the cases of

13

Kingston upon Hull and Manchester. Bournemouth Corporation decided, alone amongst operators, to sacrifice passenger capacity by installing not only a rear entrance as well as a front exit, but by providing both an up and a down staircase. Some systems were worked by four-wheelers, as happened at Llanelli, Portsmouth, St Helens and South Shields, whilst others preferred the larger six-wheelers, which normally seated 70. Belfast, Doncaster, London and Newcastle upon Tyne were examples of networks that chose these vehicles. On the other hand, both Darlington and Rotherham continued to purchase new single-deckers.

The electric motors used in the average trolleybus during the fourth decade of the twentieth century were a great deal more advanced than those previously employed. For instance, Bournemouth's Sunbeam MS2s with their BTH 101 units and Reading's AEC 661Ts with English Electric 406/3E motors were rated at 80 horsepower, whilst many of London's enormous fleet were powered by 95 horsepower Metro-Vick 206 motors.

Amongst the unusual trolleybus items to appear during the 1930s were two turntables, each located where there was not sufficient road width for a trolleybus to complete a 180 degree turn. These were situated in Christchurch (on the Bournemouth system) and at Huddersfield.

Above: *The 'utility' Sunbeam W4 belonging to Derby Corporation is seen here on an enthusiasts' tour in Allestree Lane in 1965.*

Right: *Maidstone Corporation's Sunbeam W4 number 57 received a new smarter Roe body in the 1960s.*

On the famous Christchurch turntable is Bournemouth Corporation's Sunbeam MS2 of 1934, converted into an open-topper in 1958.

THE 'UTILITY' YEARS

Throughout the period which became known as the 'Phoney War' new trolleybuses continued to be delivered and one new system, that of Cardiff, was opened, beginning public services on 1st March 1942. London Transport converted some routes in East Ham and Barking to trolleybus working on 9th June 1940 at the height of the Dunkirk crisis. Because of a shortage of vehicles the LPTB had borrowed eighteen Sunbeams from Bournemouth Corporation in December 1940, but as from November the following year these were displaced by new Leyland and AEC trolleybuses which should have been exported to either Durban or Johannesburg. These were 6 inches (152 mm) wider, at 8 feet (2.4 metres), and were designated as the board's South African classes (SA1, SA2 and SA3).

During the Blitz 61 London trolleybuses were either destroyed or else so badly damaged that they had to be given new bodies by Weymann, East Lancs or Northern Coachbuilders. Bournemouth Corporation also loaned some of its trolleybuses to Llanelli, Newcastle upon

Tyne, South Shields, Walsall and Wolverhampton: being a premier seaside resort without major war industries Bournemouth had more vehicles than it needed. Brighton was in a similar position and sent some of its AEC 661Ts up to Newcastle for a period. Neither town lost any vehicles in incidents like the one that occurred in South Shields on 30th September 1941, when incendiary bombs burnt out three trolleybuses in the market place.

In 1942 the Government allowed a limited production of a new trolleybus chassis for the home market made by Sunbeam and its subsidiary (since 1935), Karrier. This model, the W4, was powered by various makes of 85 horsepower motor and was given standard 'utility' bodywork, which included 56 wooden seats. Amongst the first operators to receive these wartime vehicles was Maidstone Corporation and their chassis carried Park Royal bodies. A few variations on this imposed uniformity were permitted. St Helens Corporation, for example, was allowed 50-seat low-bridge Charles Roe bodywork, whilst Darling-

Rotherham Corporation number 3, a Daimler CTC6 with an East Lancs central-entrance body, is seen here on a Doncaster Omnibus and Light Railway Society excursion in 1961.

ton Corporation was permitted to take delivery of 33-seat central-entrance single-deckers with bodywork by Brush. Many W4s entered service until this model was replaced by the postwar improved F4 model in 1947.

Inevitably there were reductions in timetables, especially on Sundays and late in the evening. Strict blackout regulations had to be observed with hooded headlamps and even, in some instances, tinted window glass. Flashes from the overhead wires must have been a constant worry for the Civil Defence authorities.

Nevertheless, trolleybuses had their merits since they ran on home-produced electricity made from home-extracted coal, unlike motorbuses, which relied on imported fuels.

The Mexborough and Swinton Traction Company Sunbeam F4 with Brush single-decker bodywork ended its days as a Bradford double-decker.

Nottingham City 596, a BUT 9641T, outside Nottingham's Midland railway station in 1960.

POSTWAR BOOM

In 1949 Glasgow, the tramway Mecca of Britain at that time, made a very late beginning with trolleybuses. On Sunday 3rd April a fleet of 70-seater BUT 9641Ts began route 102 between Polmadie and Riddie. This had been a tram route that had been temporarily operated by motor-buses for six weeks whilst the overhead wiring was altered to suit trolleybuses. By the time that the final route 103 was inaugurated on 16th November 1958 Glasgow Corporation had built its fleet up to 194 vehicles, including 21 single-deckers.

Already extensive networks were being expanded during the decade that followed the Second World War. Newcastle upon Tyne added a further 11 route miles (17.7 km) to its existing system. The doyen of trolleybus operators, Bradford Corporation, purchased a dozen new trolleybuses for the conversion of the old Bradford Moor tram route in 1949 and opened the Thornbury route in 1952, with the Buttershaw extension following

two years later. Portsmouth Corporation's network had a short-lived revival between 1952 and 1963 when new trolley-bus services were started in the Copnor district.

But the smaller systems were also expanding as the boom in passenger traffic continued between 1945 and the early 1950s. As late as 31st March 1968 Tees-side joined its Grangetown and Normanby routes to form a circular service. Between 1947 and 1965 Maid-stone Corporation added just over 2 more route miles (3.2 km) to the 5 that they had operated since 1930. When Brighton, Hove and District Omnibus Company began to run trolleybuses in 1944, the joint network run with Brighton Corporation was extended to Black Rock in the east (replacing a bus route) and to Carden Avenue in the north to serve new housing estates. In 1958 Bournemouth Corporation converted three of its aging Sunbeam MS2s into 69-seat open-toppers for use on the special summer circular

Ipswich Corporation 101 was a W4 which bore a Karrier manufacturer's plate.

Belfast City 199 was a BUT 9614T with local Harkness bodywork.

Bournemouth Corporation 292 was a BUT 9611T which began work in Sussex, as Brighton, Hove and District 6392.

Below: *Reading Corporation 157, a BUT 9611T, is seen here acting as the bridal 'car' for the chairman of the Reading Transport Society's wedding in 1964.*

19

Above: *Walsall Corporation 863 was a Sunbeam F4A with a distinctive sloping Willowbrook body.*

Left: *Nottingham City 803 was a trolleybus overhead tower wagon based at the Trent Bridge depot.*

Below: *Newcastle upon Tyne 490 was an 8 foot (2.4 metre) wide BUT 9641T, originally destined for London Transport, as its destination layout shows.*

Above: *Doncaster Corporation 384, a Sunbeam W4 with a Brush wartime body, began work as Southend-on-Sea Corporation 130.*

Below left: *Walsall 850, a Crossley TDD42 trolleybus, was once in the fleet of Cleethorpes Urban District Council.*

Below right: *This handsome Weymann-bodied BUT 9611T was sold by Brighton Corporation to Maidstone Corporation, which retained its fleet number, 52.*

route 39 from Bournemouth Pier, the only such service in the world.

Partly because of mergers, the number of trolleybus manufacturers was fewer in 1947 than it had been in 1937. Sunbeam and its subsidiary, Karrier, had passed into the hands of Guy Motors in 1948, whilst AEC and Leyland had joined forces in this field by building the new British United Traction chassis. English Electric had withdrawn from all but manufacturing the motors. Daimler was to abandon its CTC, CTE and CTM models in 1950. Crossley made a brief reappearance on the scene during 1950-1 with its four-wheel 'Empire' and six-wheel 'Dominion' models, which sold just 45 and 16 respectively, almost all going either to Ashton-under-Lyne Corporation or to Manchester, although a few 'Empires' were bought by Cleethorpes Urban District Council.

The gradual relaxation of regulations on the length and width of public service vehicles allowed for six-wheelers like the BUT 9641T and the Sunbeam S7 to be succeeded by the 30 foot (9.1 metre) long four-wheeled Sunbeam F4A in 1954 and the 35 foot (7.6 metre) long single-decked BUT RETB1 in 1958. Some operators specified slightly different models, such as the BUT 9612T for the Ashton-under-Lyne and Manchester fleets, the BUT 9613T for Glasgow and the Sunbeam S7A for Huddersfield.

Electric motors were becoming more powerful, mirroring the new generation of diesel units. So the postwar Q1 class of London Transport was powered by 120 horsepower Metrovick motors, Newcastle upon Tyne's final batches of trolleybuses had 120 horsepower English Electric motors and Glasgow's fleet was powered by either 115 horsepower or 120 horsepower units.

Whether by the seaside at Hastings, in a regional capital such as Belfast or Cardiff, in a country market town like Ipswich or in a large manufacturing town like Nottingham, the trolleybus flourished in the ten years that followed the end of the Second World War. These were its boom years. Yet already the seeds of its destruction had been sown.

Manchester City 1248, a Crossley 'Dominion' trolleybus, emerges from the depot.

Glasgow's BUT RETB1, number TBS13, seen in action before being preserved by the Glasgow Museum of Transport.

SWIFT DEMISE

In 1960 the future of trolleybuses looked reasonably secure, yet twelve years later buses had replaced them even on the streets of Bradford where they had been a familiar and treasured sight for over sixty years.

During the 1960s the first systems to close were those of Mexborough and Swinton in 1961 along with Brighton Corporation (that of its partner, Brighton, Hove and District Omnibus Company, having gone in 1959). By that date London Transport was in the midst of a massive replacement of its huge trolleybus network by the new 'Routemaster' diesel-engined buses. This was done in thirteen phases, the last of which took place on 8th May 1962 with the closure of Fulwell depot.

An additional factor was the power supply. Whereas in the early days of trolleybuses electricity supplies came from municipally owned power stations, and therefore helped to make passenger services profitable, since the late 1940s the electricity industry had been nationalised, causing a tremendous loss of revenue.

In 1963 the trolleybus networks in Portsmouth, Ipswich and Doncaster closed, followed in 1964 by those at South Shields and Hull. The long-standing Rotherham system ended in 1965. Yet even at that stage it looked as if a handful of systems would continue to operate. Although by 1965 trolleybus manufacture in Britain had ceased, there were sufficient good second-hand trolleybuses available to prevent a shortage of vehicles for perhaps two more decades, since the average life expectancy for a trolleybus was about twice that of a motorbus at that time. In the case of Bradford, newcomers to the fleet were rebodied to make them last longer and vehicles were taken in from Hastings, Darlington and St Helens. Cleethorpes vehicles joined the Walsall fleet and some from Brighton, Hove and District went to Bournemouth.

The decline continued, with the systems at Nottingham, Newcastle upon Tyne, Ashton-under-Lyne and Manchester closing in 1966, to be followed by Maidstone, Glasgow and Derby in 1967. At that stage there seemed to be a chance that the remaining eight systems might

The ceremonial opening of the Grangetown extension of the Tees-side system on 31st March 1968 being carried out by Sunbeam F4 number 3.

carry on indefinitely. Tees-side even opened a new route extension in 1968.

However, closures continued, and whilst the people of Grangetown and Normanby might be celebrating their new through service of trolleybuses, Belfast, Bournemouth, Huddersfield and Reading were planning to abandon their systems. Some of the newest Reading vehicles went to Tees-side to augment that fleet.

Roadworks provided further problems

Bradford Corporation 785, a Karrier W4, began life as a single-decker with Darlington Corporation. Before its new East Lancs body was fitted the chassis was lengthened.

24

The final procession of Bournemouth trolleybuses on 20th April 1969, led by Sunbeam MF2B number 278.

Below: *The last operational trolleybus depot in Britain was that at Thornbury in Bradford.*

Ipswich Corporation's Ransomes, Sims and Jefferies number 42 in a derelict state on a farm near Saxmundham in 1970.

A sister vehicle to the one above, number 44, was luckier. Here the trolleybus is being towed to London, where she is now displayed at the Science Museum.

The 1971 Sandtoft Gathering line-up, before any overhead wiring had been erected.

How different is the scene in 1986, fifteen years later, with Nottingham 578, a BUT 9641T, operating on the Inner Circle route.

for trolleybus operators. The centre of Bradford was being remodelled, whilst the new M6 motorway had cut the Walsall network into two. Diesel buses could cope with such necessary diversions, but not trolleybuses for which new standards and overhead at prohibitive costs were needed. The establishment of the Passenger Transport Executives in 1969 meant that Walsall was absorbed into the huge new West Midlands PTE, whilst Bradford found itself part of the West Yorkshire PTE. Neither of these bodies was in favour of electric transport.

Cardiff succumbed in 1970, followed by Walsall. Tees-side (soon to be merged into Cleveland Transit with local government reorganisation in 1974) ran for the last time on 4th April 1971. Ironically, it was the National Union of Mineworkers' dispute with the government during the early months of 1972 which dealt the death blow to the Bradford network. Because of frequent power cuts, service was withdrawn on 10th February 1972, although there was a final day of special runs on Sunday 26th March, when trolley 843, an ex-Mexborough and Swinton Sunbeam F4, had the honour to be the final vehicle to carry fare-paying passengers. Its sister vehicle (844) was the last trolleybus as it was the final ceremonial vehicle to enter the depot.

Fortunately teams of enthusiasts were already engaged in various projects to ensure that these interesting vehicles were restored and able to operate in new locations such as the Sandtoft Transport Centre, South Yorkshire, and the East Anglia Transport Museum, Suffolk (see 'Places to visit').

Ashton-under-Lyne Corporation 87, a BUT 9612T, being restored at the East Anglia Transport Museum at Carlton Colville in 1971.

The former Primitive Methodist chapel at Belton, which became Britain's first trolleybus museum in 1967.

A backward tow for Ipswich's Sunbeam F4 number 126 at the 1982 Sandtoft Gathering.

Front and rear views of the prototype Hestair-Dennis 'Dominator' trolleybus at Doncaster Racecourse on trials in August 1985.

REBIRTH?

In November 1983 an imported trolleybus carried out some trial runs during a conference on electric transport held in Blackpool, a town that has been so loyal to the tram that it has never needed any other form of electrically powered public transport. Hence, as with some of the earliest trolleybus trials, the vehicle used the tramway overhead. A year later, at the 1984 Commercial Motor Show, the first British-manufactured trolleybus chassis to be displayed for 26 years was on view. This had been built by Hestair-Dennis of Guildford, which in itself was remarkable since the former Dennis Brothers did not manufacture such vehicles. Basically this was a modified version of their highly successful 'Falcon' diesel bus. It had a GEC motor mounted at the rear, along with an auxiliary three-cylinder Dorman air-cooled diesel unit. This made it possible for the vehicle to move, albeit slowly, without the use of any overhead wiring, just as trolleybuses had employed their large batteries to carry out such manoeuvres in the past.

Two Passenger Transport Executives showed interest — South Yorkshire and West Yorkshire, from the heartlands of traditional trolleybus operating (five of the earliest systems had originated in Yorkshire). Although West Yorkshire was unable to obtain financial backing either from the government or from the European Economic Community, in September 1987 they decided to proceed with Stage 1 between Bradford and Buttershaw, scheduled to open in 1990.

South Yorkshire was more successful, taking delivery of the initial 'Falcon' as number 2450 (B 450 CKW). This was first demonstrated on special overhead erected at Doncaster Racecourse on 1st July 1985. Later that year it was re-registered as C 45 HDT. The next step was to promote in Parliament the South Yorkshire Transport Bill, which laid out details of routes to be run in both Doncaster and Rotherham. This duly passed through all its stages and received the royal assent. It is hoped that the first such services will begin to operate by the early 1990s.

FURTHER READING

There are books about many of the trolleybus systems that once operated in Britain, and the following list includes a few of these, along with books of more general scope.

Bilbé, D. G., et al. *100 Years of Trolleybuses.* Trolleybooks, 1982.
Bowen, D. G., and Callow, J. *The Cardiff Trolleybus.* National Trolleybus Association, 1969.
Brearley, Harold, and Beach, David T. *Under Two Liveries.* West Riding Transport Society, 1970.
Brown, T. J. *The Walsall Trolleybus System.* West Riding Transport Society, 1970.
Canneaux, T. P., and Hanson, N. H. *The Trolleybuses of Newcastle upon Tyne.* Trolleybooks, 1974.
Chalk, David L. *The Silent Service.* Omnibus Society, 1962.
Deans, Brian T. *Glasgow Trolleybuses.* Scottish Tramway Museum Society, 1966.
Jowitt, Robert T. *A Silence of Trolleybuses.* Ian Allan, 1971.
Joyce, J. *Trolleybus Trails.* Ian Allan, 1963.
Kaye, David. *British Buses and Trolleybuses Before 1919.* Blandford, 1972.
— *British Buses and Trolleybuses, 1919 to 1945.* Blandford, 1970.
— *British Buses and Trolleybuses Since 1945.* Blandford, 1968.
— *The British Bus Scene in the 1930s.* Ian Allan, 1981.
King, J. S. *Transport of Delight.* National Trolleybus Association, 1972.
Kirk, David. *London's Trolleybuses.* PSV Circle/Omnibus Society, 1969.
Leak, Michael J., et al. *The Bradford Trolleybus : 75 Years Souvenir Tribute.* Bradford Trolleybus Association, 1986.
Scotney, D. J. S. *The Maidstone Trolleybus.* National Trolleybus Association, 1972.
Whitehead, R. A. *Garretts of Leiston.* Model and Allied Publications, 1964.
York, F. W. *The Trolleybuses of Birmingham.* British Trolleybus Association, 1971.

The joint PSV Circle/Omnibus Society fleet histories (including area volumes on municipal fleets) contain much useful data. *Trolleybus* magazine and occasional articles in *Buses* also cover the subject in considerable detail.

PLACES TO VISIT

Black Country Museum, Tipton Road, Dudley, West Midlands DY1 4SQ. Telephone: 021-557 9643. Exhibits: Walsall 862 (Sunbeam F4A); Wolverhampton 433 (Sunbeam W4).

Bournemouth Transport and Rural Museum, Transport Depot, Mallard Road, Bournemouth. Telephone: 0202 21009. Exhibits: Bournemouth 202 (open-top Sunbeam MS2); Bournemouth 246 (BUT 9641T); Bournemouth 297 and 301 (Sunbeam MF2Bs).

Bradford Industrial Museum, Moorside Mills, Moorside Road, Eccleshill, Bradford BD2 3HP (but may move shortly to Saltaire). Telephone: 0274 631756. Exhibit: Bradford 737 (Karrier W4).

East Anglia Transport Museum, Chapel Road, Carlton Colville, Lowestoft, Suffolk NR33 8BL. Telephone: 0502 69399. Exhibits: Ashton-under-Lyne 80 (Crossley TDD42); Ashton-under-Lyne 87 (BUT 9612T); Brighton Corporation 52 (BUT 9611T); Brighton, Hove and District 6340 (AEC 661T); Bournemouth 286 (Sunbeam MF2B); Belfast 246 (Sunbeam F4A); Hastings 34 (Sunbeam W4); London Transport 260 (AEC 664T); London Transport 1201 and 1253 (Leyland LPTB70s); London Transport 1521 (MCW Chassisless).

Glasgow Museum of Transport, Kelvin Hall, 1 Bunhouse Road, Glasgow G3 8DP. Telephone: 041-357 3929. Exhibit: Glasgow TBS13 (BUT RETB1).

London Transport Museum, 39 Wellington Street, Covent Garden, London WC2E 7BB. Telephone: 01-379 6344. Exhibit: London United 1 (AEC 663T — a 'Diddler').

National Museum of Wales, Cathays Park, Cardiff CF1 3NP. Telephone: 0222 397951. Exhibit: Cardiff 215 (BUT 9641T).

North of England Open Air Museum, Beamish Hall, Beamish, Stanley, County Durham DH9 0RG. Telephone: 0207 231811. Exhibit: Newcastle upon Tyne 501 (Sunbeam S7).

Preston Hall Museum, Preston Park, Yarm Road, Stockton-on-Tees, Cleveland TS18 3RH. Telephone: 0642 781184. Exhibit: Tees-side 5 (Sunbeam F4).

Portsmouth Transport Museum, Eastney Depot, Highland Road, Southsea, Portsmouth, Hampshire. Telephone: 0705 822251 or 834700. Exhibit: Portsmouth 201 (AEC 661T).

Sandtoft Transport Centre, Belton Road, Sandtoft, near Doncaster, South Yorkshire. Telephone: 0302 771520. Exhibits (a selection only): Bournemouth 212 (Sunbeam MS2); Bradford 706 (Karrier W4); Cardiff 203 (AEC 664T); Cleethorpes 159 (BUT 9611T); Derby 175 (Sunbeam W4/'utility' bodywork); Doncaster 375 (Karrier W4); Glasgow TB78 (BUT 9613T); Huddersfield 619 (Sunbeam S7A); Maidstone 72 (Sunbeam W4); Manchester 1250 (Crossley TDD64); Nottingham 367 (Karrier E6); Reading 113 (AEC 661T); Rotherham 37 (Daimler CTC6 single-decker); South Shields 204 (Karrier E4); St Helens 87 (BUT 9611T); Tees-side T291 (Sunbeam F4A); Walsall 342 (Sunbeam W4).

Science Museum, Exhibition Road, South Kensington, London SW7 2DD. Telephone: 01-589 3456. Exhibit: Ipswich 44 (Ransomes, Sims and Jefferies).

Steamport Transport Museum, Derby Road, Southport, Merseyside. Telephone: 0704 30693. Exhibits: Bradford 703 and 713 (Karrier W4s).

Transport Museum Society of Ireland, Howth Castle, near Dublin. Exhibits: Belfast 183 (Guy BTX); Bournemouth 299 (Sunbeam MF2B); London Transport 1348 (Leyland LPTB70).

Ulster Folk and Transport Museum, Witham Street, Belfast BT4 1HP. Telephone: 0232 451519. Exhibits: Belfast 98 (AEC 664T); Belfast 112 (Guy BTX).

Some trolleybuses are towed to transport rallies during summer months. Readers are asked to admire vehicles from outside, unless invited on board. Please remember, too, that if you are tempted to take a souvenir away with you then the vehicle cannot be enjoyed in its entirety by other enthusiasts, and that such a loss is heartbreaking to those who may have devoted their leisure time for over four years to the restoration of the trolleybus.